# What Eats That?

## PREDATORS, PREY, AND THE FOOD CHAIN

story by **Ryan Jacobson**, photographs by **Stan Tekiela**

Adventure Publications
Cambridge, Minnesota

## Dedication

For my favorite eating buddies: Brody, Darcy, Joe, and Michelle. –Ryan Jacobson

To my lovely daughter, Abby, as she goes off into the world. –Stan Tekiela

## Acknowledgments

Special thanks to our models Ada, Jonah, and Lucas, and to the parents who let us borrow them; to my family for your honest input; and to everyone who volunteered to "test read" the book. –R

## Credits

Edited by Sandy Livoti

Cover and book design by Jonathan Norberg

All photos by Stan Tekiela except for the mosquitoes and boy with fish, used under license from Shutterstock.com. Silhouettes by Jonathan Norberg, Anthony Hertzel, and Shutterstock.

10 9 8 7 6 5 4 3

**What Eats That?**
Copyright © 2017 by Ryan Jacobson and Stan Tekiela
Published by Adventure Publications
An imprint of AdventureKEEN
310 Garfield Street South
Cambridge, Minnesota 55008
(800) 678-7006
www.adventurepublications.net
All rights reserved
Printed in China
ISBN 978-1-59193-749-4 (pbk.)

# What Eats That?

Kid

Do you know what a food chain is? Every time you eat, you are part of one. A food chain is a string of living things that eat (and might be eaten by) other living things.

Plants and animals are in many different food chains. Animals eat to fill their bellies. But while they're on the hunt, other critters might be hunting them! Let's look at a food chain and find out . . .

# What eats that?

# Flower

L: **Dame's Rocket** | R: **Ox-eye Daisy** | INSET: **Purple Fringed Orchid**

Can you guess where food chains begin? Here's a hint: It's bright, warm, and up in the sky. Yes, food chains start with the sun! Flowers and plants need sunlight to grow. It helps them to make food from air, soil, and water. So a flower needs sunlight, but . . .

## What eats that?

# Butterfly

L: **Monarch** | R: **Orange Sulphur** | INSET: **Tiger Swallowtail**

Have you ever seen a butterfly? Was it near a flower? The two go great together—and not just because they're pretty. Many flowers make a sugary liquid called nectar. Butterflies use nectar for food. They suck it out with their tongues, which work like a straw. So a butterfly feeds on nectar, but . . .

## What eats that?

# Dragonfly

Dragonflies look small to us, but they are monsters of the insect world. When they hunt, they zoom over prey and catch it in their legs. They often eat tiny bugs, like mosquitoes. But they sometimes eat bees and butterflies, too. So a dragonfly eats butterflies, but . . .

## What eats that?

# Spider

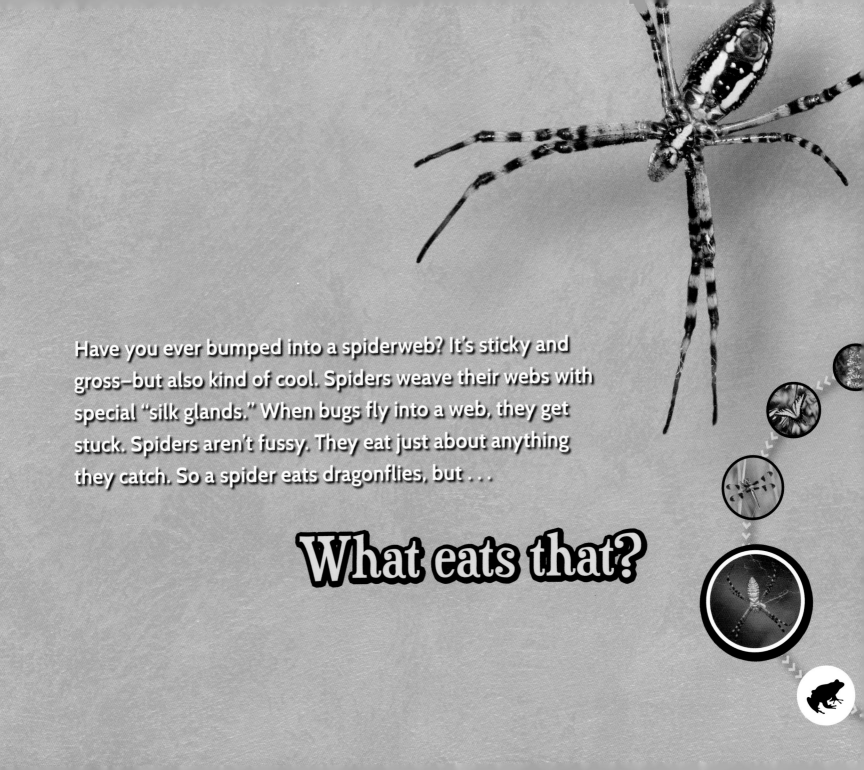

Have you ever bumped into a spiderweb? It's sticky and gross—but also kind of cool. Spiders weave their webs with special "silk glands." When bugs fly into a web, they get stuck. Spiders aren't fussy. They eat just about anything they catch. So a spider eats dragonflies, but . . .

# What eats that?

# Frog

Can you sit perfectly still? Can you stay like that for hours? That's how frogs hunt. They find a buggy spot, and they wait. When prey gets close, a frog strikes. It flips out its long, sticky tongue and grabs the prey. Then it pulls the critter into its mouth. Gulp! So a frog eats spiders, but . . .

## What eats that?

# Snake

L: **Florida Water Snake** | R: **Brown Snake** | INSET: **Smooth Green Snake**

Are you afraid of snakes? You would be if you were a small animal. Snakes find prey by sensing movement and by smelling (with their tongues). Some snakes attack with venomous bites. Some wrap their bodies around prey and squeeze. So a snake eats frogs, but . . .

# What eats that?

# Raccoon

ALL: **Northern Raccoon**

Do raccoons really eat snakes? Yes! Snakes are not a raccoon's favorite food, but the furry critters eat just about anything. Raccoons dine on animals, plants, nuts, and even garbage! If it can be chewed and swallowed, a raccoon will give it a taste. So a raccoon eats snakes, but . . .

## What eats that?

# Wolf

ALL: Gray Wolf

Wolves are big and strong, so raccoons seem like easy prey. They're not! Raccoons are fierce fighters. Plus, raccoons climb trees, and wolves cannot. Wolves hunt in packs for large animals, like elk and deer. But wolves sometimes do prey upon raccoons. So a wolf eats raccoons, but . . .

# What eats that?

# Mosquito

L: *Aedes* mosquito | R: *Culex* mosquito | INSET: *Culex* mosquito

Wolves are at the top of their food chain. No animals hunt them. But some tiny bugs feed on their blood. Female mosquitoes need animal or human blood to create eggs for their babies to hatch. Blood isn't their favorite food, though. Mosquitoes prefer nectar, just like butterflies. So a mosquito sips wolf blood, but . . .

**What eats that?**

# Fish

L: **Smallmouth Bass** | R: **Yellow Perch** | INSET: **Smallmouth Bass**

Wait! Fish live underwater, and mosquitoes fly above it. How can fish eat them? Well, mosquitoes lay eggs in wet places. After the eggs hatch, baby mosquitoes–called mosquito larvae–live in the water. These larvae are a perfect meal for fish. So a fish eats mosquito larvae, but . . .

## What eats that?

Kid

Have you ever gone fishing? Some people catch fish just for fun. They throw their catches back in the water. Others keep their fish for dinner. Yum! Which would you do: eat it or throw it back?

Fish is just one kind of food for people. What are your favorite foods to eat?

# Food Chains

There are many different food chains—too many to count. For example, lots of critters eat mosquitoes. Take a look at the food chains on the next page.

**JUST FOR FUN:** Work with a grown-up to make a food chain that includes your favorite animal!

# Other Mosquito Food Chains:

Mosquito >>> Bat >>> Owl

Mosquito >>> Bird >>> Raccoon >>> Cougar

Mosquito >>> Fish >>> Otter >>> Alligator

Mosquito >>> Frog >>> Opossum >>> Fisher

# What else do they eat?

### Butterfly
Butterflies don't really "eat." They drink liquids. Along with nectar from flowers, butterflies sip on water, juices from rotten fruits, and tree sap.

### Dragonfly
Dragonflies usually consume small insects, such as mosquitoes. They have also been known to prey upon insects as large as bees, butterflies, and wasps.

### Spider
Spiders make meals out of bugs and other spiders. In some parts of the world, the largest spiders might gobble up frogs and small birds.

### Frog
Frogs feast on all sorts of different bugs, including dragonflies, flies, and mosquitoes. Larger frogs can eat larger bugs, like grasshoppers, and worms.

## Snake

Snakes come in all sizes. Most snakes feed on bugs and small critters, such as mice and birds. The largest snakes in the world can consume animals as big as a deer.

## Raccoon

Raccoons munch on everything from fruit, nuts, and animal eggs to garbage. They eat small animals, too, like fish, mice, bats, and baby rabbits.

## Wolf

Wolves live in packs and usually hunt for large animals, like deer, elk, and moose. They might also prey upon beavers, rabbits, raccoons, and other smaller critters.

## Mosquito

Mosquitoes drink nectar from plants. The females also need blood from animals—or people—in order to create eggs.

## Fish

Fish can only feed on plants and animals found on or in water. That includes bugs and other fish. Large fish might dine on frogs and young water birds.

## About the Author

Ryan Jacobson is an author and presenter. He has written more than 40 books, priding himself on telling high-interest stories for each age level. He can talk picture books in kindergarten, ghost stories in eighth grade, and other fun stuff in between. Ryan has performed at countless schools and special events. For more about the author, visit AuthorRyanJacobson.com.

## About the Photographer

Stan Tekiela is an award-winning naturalist, wildlife photographer, and the originator of many popular state-specific field guides. He has authored more than 175 field guides, nature books, children's books, puzzles, playing cards, and more, presenting many species of birds, mammals, reptiles, amphibians, trees, wildflowers, and cacti. Stan can be followed on Facebook and Twitter and contacted via www.naturesmart.com.